I0004651

Google Drive

Beginner's Crash Course To Google Drive

(Docs, Excel, Cloud, Picture, and Video Storage)

by Jacob Simmons

Table of Contents

Disclaimer

While all attempts have been made to verify the information provided in this book, the author does not assume any responsibility for errors, omissions, or contrary interpretations of the subject matter contained within. The information provided in this book is for educational and entertainment purposes only. The reader is responsible for his or her own actions and the author does not accept any responsibilities for any liabilities or damages, real or perceived, resulting from the use of this information.

Introduction

Google Drive and its associated apps represent perhaps the purest and fullest representation of the promise of cloud computing on the market today. With apps for word processing, spread sheets, photo storage, editing, slideshows and more, Google Apps provides users with the opportunity work on any number of projects, all without having to save a thing on your own hard drive and the ability share and collaborate on your work with team members around the world.

In this guide, we'll be giving you an overview of Drive and all the different apps that connect with it. We'll be walking you through the different features of the apps and what they can be used for, as well as offering some tips for going just a bit beyond the basics.

Speaking of basics, if you don't have a Google account yet, you will need one. Before we get into the meat of things, let's walk through that process.

First step is to go to www.google.com. With that done, look in the top right for the Log In button. Click that and hit Create Account. That will bring up a standard profile page that requires your name, birthday, and of course your username and password. If you want, you can also include a phone number. That will allow Google to confirm various account actions with you by sending you verification codes via text. Once that is all done, agree to the terms of service and you will be good to go. Gmail and all the Drive apps we'll be discussing below will be at your fingertips.

Chapter 1 – Google Drive

Drive itself is Google's entry into the cloud storage realm. Offering up to 15GB of free storage, Drive is a simple, low cost way to share your files in a way that is simple and intuitive for you and your team members to use. Compared to its closest competitors, Dropbox (2GB free), OneDrive (5GB free) and iCloud (5GB free), Drive offers considerably more storage in a simpler, more useful interface.

The comparatively greater usability is due largely to the fact that there are so many other Google Apps that can be used in conjunction with it. Having apps like Docs, Sheets, and Forms makes integrating your work with Drive a simple matter.

Combined with the fact that Google is also the originator of the Android operating system and that Google has put forth the effort to ensure that its apps are compatible with the ubiquitous MS Office, means that Drive can be used easily on your mobile device or PC without having to do any file conversions on the fly. Dropbox by contrast is strictly a cloud storage app, with no other applications that work directly with it.

iCloud works well with Apple's suite of apps but has the disadvantage of being tied too heavily to them, meaning that sharing files may be more difficult in general and it may also be difficult to access those files without converting them into a different, more accessible format. Add in the fact that Apple's products tend to cost a bit more and Cupertino is at a distinct disadvantage.

But enough of these comparisons. You aren't here to be sold a free product, you're here to learn how to use it. So let's start talking about some of Drive's specific features and how to use them.

Getting There

If you use Google's Chrome browser, then getting to Drive is easy. Just open the browser go to the grid near the top right. Select Google Drive (a three colored triangle) and the program will open up. There is also a multicolored grid in the top left that does the same thing.

If you are using another browser, such as Microsoft's Edge, then you will need to go to www.google.com and click on the grid pattern towards the top right e of the browser. From there, simply select the Drive icon and you will be ready to get started.

A third option is to download the app for your computer. You will need to do this directly from Google as the app is not in the Microsoft Store. For some reason, the tech overlords at Google bury this a little bit. As of this writing, the link is: www.google.com/drive/download. Once you have downloaded the app from Google, there will be a shortcut on your desktop that allows you to open the Drive like a regular folder on your hard drive. I like to keep mine right there on the desktop for easy access.

From there you will be able to drag and drop files in and out as you wish. Those files automatically sync with your Drive, giving you instant accessibility on any device.

Now that we know how to get to the Drive in the first place, let's start taking a look at how to navigate through the app.

Top Toolbar

Search – When you open the app in your browser you will find that there is a handy search bar at the top, just under your bookmarks bar. This is really self-explanatory as it simply allows you to quickly search your drive. Search is especially useful if you are looking for an old file or if you are just generally bad at organizing them.

Apps – Next to the Search bar is Google's standard grid pattern that allows you to quickly switch to other apps in the Google stable.

Notifications – Google's standard alarm bell notification icon is also present, letting you know who has seen, shared, or edited the projects you are collaborating on, as well as all of your other Google Plus notifications.

Profile – This is simply Google's standard profile button with access to your settings and the ability to open up other accounts. I find this particularly useful as I have multiple Google accounts that I access for different purposes.

New – This button allows you to upload a file, create a new folder, or create new documents and perform a number of other activities. You can also open several other Google Apps from this button. When clicking on the desired app, it will open in a new browser tab and your work will automatically save to your drive.

Apps that can be opened include:

- Docs
- Sheets
- Slides
- Maps
- Forms
- Drawings

Other apps can also be connected to your Drive. By clicking on the "Connect more apps" option in the dropdown, you can add third party photo editors, zip extractors and more.

My Drive – This button just to the right of the "New" button performs many of the same functions as the New button.

View – This button is just below the standard Google Grid and simply allows you to toggle between 'List' and 'Grid' view.

Details – The little 'I' in the grayed out circle allows you to decide whether or not to show simple details on your projects such as the project owner and last date it was modified. The other view shows activity in the Drive such as uploads and when things are moved to the trash.

Settings – The standard gear icon opens up general information about the app, certain viewing options and more. You can also manage how notifications are handled and what apps are connected. There is also a handy list of keyboard shortcuts to improve your productivity.

Left Sidebar

Here, you can navigate to your Drive contents, files others have shared with you, and go through recent, starred, and trashed projects.

Storage can also be upgraded, allowing you to choose between the various paid plans that Google offers. $2 a month will get you a 100GB of storage and $10 a month will grant you 1TB of storage, which should be enough for nearly anyone.

The sidebar also allows access to any photos that you added to the Google Photos app. We'll discuss later how you place the images directly into Photos from Drive. Either way, it can take a minute or two to sync.

Finally, there is also a link to any backups of files on your device that you may have made.

Center Viewing Area

This area has a number of productivity enhancing features.

The top has a Quick Access section that displays the four most recent files you've worked on. Directly below this is the Folders area which allows you to navigate to any folders that you have created in your Drive.

Directly below that is all the other files, folders, and other projects that you have uploaded to your Drive. Remember, you can switch between a list and grid view using the toggle in the toolbar.

When you click on your project though, this section does get more interesting. When you do so, a number of other options show up in the toolbar. Options included are:

- Shareable Link – This provides a link to the project you want to share via email.

- Share – The Google Plus icon allows you to share your project directly with anyone via the social network.

- Preview – Does exactly what it says.

- Remove – A little trash icon that is pretty self-explanatory.

- More options – The standard three dot "wait, there's more" icon provides other actions such as opening the project with another app, renaming it, moving it, or downloading it to your hard drive.

Right clicking on your project will also bring up all of these same options in a single dropdown menu.

Right Sidebar

With a project selected, you can click on the Information button previously discussed. This will activate the right sidebar. In this space, you will find a slightly larger thumbnail of your project than you see in grid view and a host of standard information about the project such as the file size, location and when it was last modified. You can also add a more detailed description if you wish.

Now that we have thoroughly gone through Google Drive, let's move onto another Google App, one we have already briefly touched on, namely Photos.

Tips

If you are looking for a needle in your haystack of image files, and can't remember when it was taken or what you might have named it, there is help for you. Type a simple description of the image into the search box and all of your related files should come up. You may still have a lot to search through, but at least it will be narrowed down.

If Drive is installed on your phone, you can take a picture of any document and it will be stored as a PDF file.

Chapter 2 – Google Photos

Google's cloud based photo storage app looks simple when you first open it. To do that, go to the grid that I mentioned in the Drive discussion and click on the weird looking, rainbow throwing star thing that Google for some reason chose to represent its Photo app.

That will open it directly in your browser. If you are a first time user and have not uploaded anything to your Drive or Photo app before, then what you will see is mostly just white space. But there are a few buttons that reveal quickly that the bland appearance of the app is quite deceiving. As before, we'll start at the top and work our way down.

Main Menu

The three little lines to left of where "Photos" appears on screen opens up the main menu which will serve as our window into the app as a whole.

- Photos – This simply allows you to see all of your photos and videos.

- Albums – Albums will allow a user to browse and sort images and videos, with already created albums including Shared, People, Places, Things, Videos, Collages, Animations, and Movies. Naturally, you can create new albums and reorganize as you prefere.

- Assistant – The third item in the menu opens up a collection of wizards that will help you create and share albums, collages, and even animations out of the photos and other images that you have uploaded to the cloud. There will be a bit more on those below.

- Sharing – Takes you directly to all of your shared content, including things that you have shared via text.

- Photo Books – This is a new feature that lets you create physical books recording your adventures. Simply select photos from your albums to get started. Once your photos are selected, you can then go in an select how much of the page you want each photo to fill the page and go to cart to choose soft or hardcover. There aren't a lot of customization options but if you all you want is a quick photo journal of your vacation, this is a great, low-cost option.

- Archive – If a lot of photos are in the way but you don't quite have the heart to delete them, move them here. They won't clutter your main work space and will still be available when you feel the need for a stroll down memory lane.

- Trash – Again, self-explanatory.

- Add Partner Account – If you want to directly link different Google Photo accounts, this is the easisest way to do so. You can also share it with friends and family.

- Settings – The settings menu has many features that you will likely want to explore. The first lets you choose what quality you want the app to store your images in. If you choose 'Original,' the storage space will count against your free 15GB of space that comes with your Google account. However, if you choose 'High Quality' the storage space for your images is unlimited. You only get one guess as to which option has the "higher quality." There are other features that can be toggled on and off such as:

- ✓ Group Similar Faces – Automatically arranges photos with the same people into separate folders.
- ✓ Google Drive – Links the videos and photos uploaded to Drive with the Photos app.
- ✓ Remove Geolocation – This removes any information stored in the photo regarding where you were when it was taken from shared photos. This is under the Sharing drop down.
- ✓ Activity log – This lets you see and get rid of any inappropriate comments from any shared photos.

- Send Feedback – Allows the user to send detailed feedback about problems with the app, including a screenshot so you don't have to worry about copying down a complicated error code.
- Help – Opens up a searchable Help menu full of useful 'How To' articles.
- App Downloads – Last in the main menu is a link to download Google's uploader to its photo storage vault.

You will also find the Assistant, Photos, Albums, and other buttons on the left side of the window.

Top Toolbar

Again, along the top of the window is a toolbar that comes with a search bar, a create button, which includes links to create new albums, movies, etc. There is also a button to upload new files from your device.

Movies – There are a number of preselected templates that this portion of the app will work with. For example, click on the Selfie Movie and it will make a quick slideshow set to music of every selfie/portrait in your library. Other templates are a bit more customizable as they let you choose a focus for your short film.

Collage – This one is potentially a lot of fun. Working from your albums, you can select a number of images to turn into one big collage. Once created, your collage can be edited in the same way as a photo (see below) and then put into an album, photo book, or shared among friends.

Animation – This tool would be great for people wanting to get their feet wet doing stop-motion animation movies. It works like the others, by selecting a bunch of photos and letting the app turn it into an animation. Obviously, you would need to do a lot of work up front to make it effective, but it that sounds like fun, Google has an easy tool for you to use.

The Photo

So what happens when you actually select a photo? Again, for a free program, the options here are pretty impressive. Google's generous features allow you to apply several filters, zoom in and out, crop, rotate and adjust the color and light balance. The Crop and Rotate tool also allows you to also adjust the aspect ratio to make sure you get your image in the format you want. It's no Photoshop, but it's enough to give you some simple and easy to use tools to get more out of your photos.

The videos are not nearly as customizable, so they the don't really warrant their own section. You are, however, able to view your location data and easily share your videos from the app.

Tips

When you hover over a video in the main work area, it will play while your cursor is over it, giving you a preview and refreshing your memory as to its content.

Chapter 3 – Google Docs

The apps icon also allows you to go straight to Google Docs. You can also get there from inside the Drive by selecting the My Drive button and selecting Google Docs from the dropdown. This cloud based app makes it easy to create, share, and edit new documents such as stories, scripts and more. There are also templates for things like resumes, reports, and project proposals.

The opening page gives you access to all of these templates, as well as thumbnails of all the documents that you have created or have been shared with you. Options are available to display only those owned by yourself, buy others, or all, as well as whether to show them in list or grid view.

They can also be arranged by the person who modified them and when. Finally, if you have a number of folders, you can click on the folder icon to browse the folders and open up the file of your choice.

Clicking on 'Blank' opens up a blank page and toolbar that is very similar to the one you would find in Microsoft Word.

In the toolbar you will find standard options to adjust the font size and style, add text effects like underlining and highlighting, adjusting spacing, and text alignment and formatting. There is even an editing tool that will make it easy for your collaborators to see any changes that you may have made.

Clicking on the dropdown arrows all the way to the right brings up a number of other dropdown menus:

- File – Standard options like creating a new document or opening an existing one. There are also options to print, change the language, download or rename the document, and even publish directly to the internet.

- Edit – Again, standard options like cut, paste, undo, redo.

- View – Simple options like the default view, ruler, equations and spelling suggestions.

- Insert – This dropdown allows you to insert equations, images, links, charts, drawings, tables, footnotes, special characters and more. This is also where you go to insert page breaks, page headers and footers as well as creating a table of contents for your document.

- Format – Options that duplicate the settings in the default toolbar. There are also simple photo editing options like image cropping.

- Tools – Here you will find spell check, word count, voice to text, a dictionary and more.

- Table – All the options you need to insert and build a table.

- Add-ons – This gives you a link to several third party extensions for calculators, different font designs and even music notation.

- Help – Simple ways to report issues and find keyboard shortcuts.

- Comments – The Open Comments button is located to the right, next to the Share button. This isn't a dropdown but rather a button that allows you to view any comments on the document and displays any relevant notifications.

- Share – Button that allows you to share while preventing others from sharing the document.

Tips

By using the 'Share Screen' feature in Hangouts, you can share any open window with collaborators around the world.

Using the Explore option in the Tools menu will help you find websites and images related to your topic to help you flesh out your content with additional sources.

Chapter 4 – Google Sheets

Sheets, Google's answer to Microsoft's Excel spreadsheet program boasts an interface on its main page that is very similar to Docs. Just as with the word processing program, Sheets displays any existing spreadsheets that have been created and/or shared as well as multiple templates that you can choose from.

These templates are divided into in 'Personal,' 'Work,' 'Project Management', and 'Education' groups and include everything from wedding planners and calendars to invoices and grade books. As before, we'll open up a blank spreadsheet and walk through some of the available features.

Upon opening the app, you will be greeted with the familiar grid view and full-featured toolbar and set of dropdown menus.

The options offered are similar to those in Docs with the exception that there are many more that of course are tailored to creating a spreadsheet. There are options to add and delete rows as well as various calculation tools that will help you manage and understand your personal and business data.

- File – Nothing new here.
- Edit – Standard options plus the ability to delete selected rows and columns.
- View – Allows for the views of formulas, grids and ranges.
- Insert – Ability to add new rows, columns, functions and other standard options such as images.

- Format – The format drop down has tandard options for formatting fonts and text. It also boasts options to select different colors for your cells

- Data – This dropdown lets you sort your information, select and even create filers.

- Tools – Provides things like a script editor, form creation, and a personal dictionary.

- Add-ons – Just as with Docs, this gives you a link to several third party apps.

- Help – Again, nothing new here.

Tips

By selecting a set of cells and/or columns Sheets will give the user instant summaries of data.

By clicking the 123 icon, and selecting More Formats and More Currencies you can convert your currencies into foreign units.

Chapter 5 – Google Slides

Just as Sheets is Googles answer to Excel, so Slides is Google's answer to PowerPoint. And as Google does so well, they have once again designed the interface to be very like that of Sheets and Docs.

The templates are also broken down into simple Education, Work, and Personal sections. They provide a good starting point for your photo album, case study, science fair project, and much more. Once again, for anyone who has used PowerPoint, the interface will be very easy to get used to.

Top Toolbar

The quick access toolbar provides basic magnification and undo tools. There are also a number of other, much more interesting and useful options.

- Plus sign – This button allows you to add a slide and choose a layout from a dropdown menu at the same time.

- Text box – Insert a text box of any size.

- Insert image – This allows you to drag and drop images into place from your hard drive or Google Drive. It is also possible to add images via URL.

- Shapes – Functions to add in any geometric shape, arrows, speech bubbles, and mathematical symbols.

- Background – A popup window appears, allowing you to choose the background color image for each individual slide in your presentation.

- Layout – This dropdown allows you to choose where your main text boxes, headers, and sidebars are located.

- Theme – If you are not interested in completely building your presentation from the ground up, you can simply choose a theme which will provide you with a default layout, color, and font so you can get to the important business of building your presentation before the deadline hits. Previews of the different themes are available in the sidebar to the right.

- Transitions – To help liven up your presentation, Slides has a small selection of transition animations. There are not many to choose from but it does grant you the ability to apply a different transition to each slide or one to all. These also are selected on the right sidebar.

Dropdowns

Given that most of the dropdown menus have the same functions as other apps, we'll only focus on those that are more unique or relevant to Slides.

- Insert – In addition to the options provided for in the quick access toolbar, the insert menu also makes it easy to add in videos, links, charts, and animations.

- Slide – In addition to adding or copying a slide, this menu provides the ability to change backgrounds and themes.

- Format – Provides options to crop images, and change the fill color of your slide.

- Arrange – Allows you to move your images, text boxes, etc. around on your slide for maximum customizability.

Work Areas

The left sidebar allows you to scroll through thumbnails of all of your slides, making it a simple matter to find that one slide you think needs a little extra work. You can also add slides with the Plus button just above it in the toolbar or use your mouse to rearrange the slides as you see fit.

Right clicking on the thumbnails allows you to quickly cut, paste or add a slide. From here you can even change the theme, background or transitions.

The primary work area in the middle of the screen is of course where you will get most of your work done. You can rearrange the various text boxes, drag and drop images and resize them, all with your mouse, stylus or finger, depending on what device you are working on. Below your slide is also a space to add notes to help the presenter go beyond a few simple bullet points.

The right sidebar only appears when you are working with certain features such as transitions and themes as previously discussed.

Presenter Mode

Between the Comments and Share buttons in the top right is a Present button. This button takes the presentation you have open and puts it directly into the presentation format. I bring this up because if you move your cursor to the bottom left, you will get a small toolbar with some options to help you navigate.

There are of course buttons to play the whole presentation, move ahead slide by slide, or select specific slides as the need arises. More interesting is the Q&A button. This opens up a window with a link that the audience can use to send you questions. Those questions can even be viewed by the rest of the audience, saving you from having to filter several versions of the same question.

Also available are speaker notes, a timer to let you – and everyone else – know how long you've been going for. Finally, the Settings gear lets you choose to output the presentation in PDF, Powerpoint, or even print formats.

Tips

Slides actually has a built-in laser pointer. Clicking the Present button, you will find the Laser Pointer option which turns your mouse cursor into a red dot like a laser pointer.

By going to Presenter View and Audience Tools you can set up a question and answer mode that encourages audience participation.

Chapter 6 – Google Forms

Google Forms allows a user to quickly and easily create quizzes, worksheets, signup forms, invitations and more. If you go into it through My Drive, it will open up the last kind of form you were working on as default. If that is not what you are looking for, just navigate out by hitting the arrow in the top left. As the interface duplicates that of the other apps already discussed, we'll jump straight into understanding the basic format of the blank form and discussing the various tools and features that will help you to create a fully customized form. As before, we'll start at the top and work our way down.

Color Palette

There, you will find something that looks like an artist palette. Clicking on this will allow you to change the base color of the top of the form. The Palette doesn't have the kind of subtlety that you might expect if you are used to MS Office but it's adequate for most situations.

You can also add images either from a number of pre-loaded themes, upload one from your hard drive or from your Google Drive albums.

The one thing to keep in mind is that images that can be added need to be between 800x200 and 2500x2500 pixels in size to be able to fit within the document header.

Send

This button opens up a pop-up with options to send a form via email, a shared link or you can share it via Google Plus, Facebook or Twitter.

But Wait, There's More!

Those suggestive three little dots as usual contain many more options to help you quickly create and edit your forms.

Most of these options are standard. Things like Preview, Trash, Copy, and Print are available. There is also a link to allow users to report problems with the app.

The Settings menu is the most interesting here as it is possible to require others to sign in before opening the form and whether they can edit the form or read only. It is also possible to display a progress bar, alter the question order, show other links, and create your customized message that gets sent out when the completed form is submitted.

If you are creating a quiz, then settings are available that allow the person taking it to see her grade, missed questions, answers she got right and the point value associated with each question.

Main Work Area

This area is where you of course go about building your form. It is divided into two primary sections, Questions and Responses.

Questions

Here you can title and type out a general description of your form. Below that, you can begin adding questions. Using the dropdown on the right you can choose what form you want answers to be given in. Options include multiple choice, paragraph and checkboxes.

Images can also be dropped in to go with your questions.

Responses

This section allows you to track individual responses to your form, determine where you want them sent, set email notifications, or send them to a spreadsheet so that you can track and analyze them.

Right Toolbar

Unlike the other apps discussed, there is a quick access toolbar located at the right of your work area.

In order, these buttons allow the user to:

- Add a question
- Add a title and description
- Add an image
- Add a video
- Add a new section to your form.

Tips

Need more responses? Don't actually feel like spamming the people in your contacts list? Then take your form, go to File, then Embed, and then copy and paste the HTML into your website.

If you are collecting data over a period of time, you may find the ability for responders to edit their responses useful. Just click the option at the bottom of the screen when you create a new form.

Chapter 7 – Google Drawings

Unlike the above apps, this does not have a set of templates to choose from. In fact, of all the rest of the Google Apps discussed so far, this one seems the most under developed app in the Google stable. There is simply a blank work area into which can be inserted shapes, text boxes and images of various kinds.

There is also a great deal of flexibility when it comes to adding and manipulating text. However, there is no free form drawing function in the app, making the name of "Drawings' seem rather nonsensical. However, Google never leaves anything alone, so be sure to keep an eye on the app to see how it develops.

Chapter 8 – Google MyMaps

At a glance, this app clearly makes up for the relative disappointment that is Drawings. It opens up to a world map that you can use to plan routes, add markers, and more. Naturally, though, you are not likely to be travelling around the world (though you might).

And even if you are, you will want to get a little bit closer than a view from orbit in order to plan your trip. Fortunately, this app lets you do that with relative ease.

Planning a trip.

Start by going to the search bar and type in a destination. Let's say part of your trip will include Toronto, Canada. Type that into the search bar and the map will center on the city. Since Toronto is a large city, the view is still fairly far out. You can zoom in though using the buttons on the bottom right of the window, or simply by scrolling with your mouse.

Doing this, you can zoom in far enough to see markers for individual businesses and small residential roads. This can come in particularly handy if you are trying to find places to stay or eat while visiting an unfamiliar area.

Navigation is simple as well. Once you have zoomed in, you can just move the map around with your mouse, noting all the streets and attractions you will want to go to. We'll continue down our hypothetical trip.

Say you want to stay at the Chelsea Hotel in Toronto, a hotel you discovered just by zooming in on the city. By clicking on the icon, basic information like address, phone number, website and average review score show up. If you click on the website, it will take you straight there so you can research nights available, amenities, and rates.

A quick glance shows that if you want a decent cup of coffee there is a Starbucks just a few blocks down the road. And just one block down is Elmwood Spa if you want to really take a day off. You will also see nearby restaurants and even a park, all within walking distance.

Naturally though, you will want to get out of the immediate area and see some other things in the city. Let's just say that you are a hockey fan and part of the reason that you want to go to Toronto is to visit the Hockey Hall of Fame. Using the line drawing tool, you can draw out your route, setting checkpoints along the way.

You can type in directions for your route as well as get an idea of how far you will need to be travelling (if you are thinking of renting a bike instead of taking the Metro for example), you can trace your route with the ruler tool that will tell you how far the distance of each leg of your journey will be.

You can also add a title to your route and add an image to make it easy to remember what you were planning on doing on each day of your trip.

You then notice that there is a ferry terminal nearby that will take you out to some of the beautiful island parks just off the shore in Lake Ontario. The process can be repeated as many times as you like and you can even add different layers to the map so that you can plan each day individually.

And of course, since this is a Google app it is easy to share with others who might be joining you on your trip.

Correcting an old weakness, you can now find and print directions within the app. Under the search bar is an option to Add Directions which you do same as with any similar app. Once done, select the option to display step by step directions. Right clicking on the directions will bring up options to Save, Print, and even Cast them to another device.

Another strength is that it is possible to change the basic format of the map, going from the default road map, to satellite, to topographical and more. This is accomplished by selecting the Base Map drop down at the bottom of the information window in the top left.

It is also possible to u use the app to import data from the internet or Google Earth with the Import button in the same window.

There are of course other uses for MyMaps. They can be used to create virtual tours and also for educational purposes, such as showing the movement of different populations or researching concentrations of different industries, all at just a glance.

Chapter 9 – Other Apps

As previously stated, it is possible to connect a number of third party apps to your Google Drive.

Some of these are:

- DocHub – PDF editor

- MindMup – Mind map for brainstorming books and projects.

- Flat – Music composition

- WeVideo – Video Editor and Maker

- Pixlr Editor – Photo editor

- Drive Notepad – Simple note taking app

- Game Emulator with Google Drive – Emulator for SNES, NES, GameBoy and Sega Mega games. So you can relive your childhood during your breaks.

- GeoGebra Math – Graphing calculator

- PowToon – Presentations creation. Great for making educational YouTube videos.

There are literally dozens more to choose from. You are only limited by how much time you have to spend exploring the various options and determining which will work best for your needs.

Conclusion

Google Drive and its associated apps represent the best in modern cloud computing. With the ability to create, edit, store, and share nearly any project, it is also one of the most versatile. From slideshows, to trip planning, to writing that report that needs to be on the boss' desk in two days, Google Apps does almost anything that anyone could need.

While there are a couple of weak points in the software that we have discussed, it is hard to complain too much since Google provides Drive and the rest for free.

Add in the fact that Google is always developing new tools and tweaking old ones, it is very easy to see why so many people have turned to Google for their cloud computing needs.

www.ingramcontent.com/pod-product-compliance
Lightning Source LLC
Chambersburg PA
CBHW060935050326
40689CB00013B/3107